What they're saying about *Surviving Your Feelings*

Dennis C. Stager's "Cannot Preach, Cannot Teach, Must Reach" philosophy combines with an earlier philosophy that I carry with me. It states that every subordinate will perform to their highest capability if you give them adequate training and time for the job, the correct tools to do the job, and you leave them alone to work without overseeing every movement. Next, you make them feel wanted and appreciated, then allow them to perform and discuss their work after it is completed.

On my walk through the Honor Guards with my wife, acknowledging my final military salute after the officiant sent me ashore, I realized I had survived a career in the military and never regretted a day served. Among the super people I will never forget were Captain Ivan E. Hughes and Senior Chief Dennis C. Stager.

Now, at age 85, I understand that managing and surviving my feelings has been the driving force of my long life. Listen to your feelings when they speak. They are telling you something you should heed. So, look around and seek tested answers to the questions these feelings initiate. Heads up, brain in gear, and forward march.

CDR George McKinney
United States Navy (Ret.)

Surviving Your Feelings

Deal with your emotions and proceed with the light of freedom

Dennis C. Stager

Aviation Electronics Tech, Senior CPO, United States Navy (Ret.)

Surviving Your Feelings
By Dennis C. Stager
© 2024 by Dennis C. Stager. All rights reserved.

Editing by Adam Colwell's WriteWorks, LLC, Adam Colwell and Ginger Colwell
Cover and interior design by Ink to Book
Published by the author through Kindle Direct Publishing
Printed in the United States of America
Paperback ISBN: 979-8-9885033-8-5
Hardcover ISBN: 979-8-9885033-9-2
eBook ISBN: 979-8-9900002-0-9

All rights reserved. Except in the case of brief quotations embodied in critical articles and reviews, no portion of this book may be reproduced, stored in a retrieval system, or transmitted in any form or by any means—electronic, mechanical, photocopy, recording, scanning, or other—without the prior written permission from the author. None of the material in this book may be reproduced for any commercial promotion, advertising or sale of a product or service.

While the author has made every effort to provide accurate internet addresses at the time of publication, neither the publisher nor the author assumes any responsibility for errors or for changes that occur after publication. Further, the publisher does not have any control over and does not assume any responsibility for author or third-party websites or their content.

Table of Contents

Dedication   vii

Foreword: Navy Captain Ivan E. Hughes (Ret.)   ix

Introduction: Surviving the Battle with Emotions   xvii

1	A Place to Start	1
2	Nah, Don't Take My Word for It. Test "It."	7
3	Surviving "Your" Feelings	13
4	Using Skill to Build a New Tool Box	17
5	Results of Using Tested Life Tools	21
6	The Monster "It"	25
7	Life's Lie	27
8	The Upward Ladder	31
9	Running From Life's Little Demons	35

10	LIFE'S BUCKET OF PAIN	41
11	THE EMOTIONAL BUCKET	47
12	ALL OF US DEAL WITH IT	51
13	COUNTER THE EMOTIONAL HYPE	55
14	BELONGING	61
15	TRUTH: THE WAY TO TRUE BELONGING	67
16	FACILITATED GROWTH	71
17	ANNOTATE AND IDENTIFY THE TRIGGERS	77
18	DISARMING THE EXPLOSIVE GARBAGE CAN	81
19	BUILDING BLOCKS OR ROADBLOCKS?	85
20	THE CAFETERIA OF LIFE	89
21	FREEDOM WITH RESPONSIBILITY	93
ABOUT THE AUTHOR		97

Dedication

This book could not have become a venue for truths without input from the hundreds of people who've attended and contributed to my "Surviving Your Feelings" presentations. A real and perhaps most important credit goes to Navy Captain Ivan E. Hughes (Ret.), who sanctioned my job as his human resources officer. That job, one I never wanted, turned into the best job I've ever had. I learned more than anyone else there.

May all of you, in all walks of life, continue to use the life tools and treasures of your experiences. I am most grateful for your open friendship and visible honesty, and I remain armed with your integrity.

May God richly bless your every honest endeavor.

Finally, everyone in a successful leadership or teaching role must have someone they can trust absolutely, no question about it, 24/7. This person will be there for you to lean upon and walk the path that solves problems. This person must be strong enough to hold you up during the tough times and sensitive enough to enjoy your successes.

For me, that person is my girlfriend of 60-plus years, Virginia. She is the finest lady I've ever known. She is also my wife of 60 years. Many successes I have obtained were guided by her sound advice. The best co-pilot I've ever flown beside, she exhibits, for me, love that enables the "decision to care" and is the backbone that helps me to stand tall at all times.

Thank you, Virginia.

Foreword

Far Better Shape

Navy Captain Ivan E. Hughes (Ret.)

In my nearly 32 years of service in the United States Navy, I served with at least a few thousand people from all walks of life. Each one was blessed (or cursed) with their own belief systems which informed, and sometimes dictated, the manner in which they faced the daily trials and tribulations of military life. One such individual, whose great service helped me come to grips with the most difficult assignment of my entire career, is Dennis

Surviving Your Feelings

C. Stager—and I am very proud that he asked me to write the Foreword to this book.

I was screened for command in late 1980. Shortly after being informed that I was to be a squadron commander, I was told that I would be assigned to Fleet Air Reconnaissance Squadron One (VQ-1) based on Guam. This was an immediate red flag to me because the billet for the command of VQ-1 had been for a captain (0-6) since 1967, and I was still a commander (0-5). Another issue that gave me a great amount of concern was that an old friend of mine, Commander Chuck Templin, had been slated to be commanding officer of the squadron, but Chuck had been fired (relieved for cause) by the current captain who commanded the VQ-1.

Over the next four months. I refused to accept the orders to Guam as I consulted with every senior officer I knew who had an understanding of what had happened there to warrant the firing of my friend, Chuck. Knowing him and his quiet, reserved ways, I began to think that if Chuck could have done something that got him fired after only a few months as executive officer, I wouldn't last two weeks before

Far Better Shape: Navy Captain Ivan E. Hughes (Ret.)

I was canned from the job. I wasn't anything like Chuck, and my personality wasn't anything close to "quiet and reserved." Some would say the expression in the motion picture, Top Gun, of "going Mach two with his hair on fire" fit me to a tee!

When I finally told the Navy that I would accept the orders to Guam on March 30, 1981, (the day of the assassination attempt on President Ronald Reagan), I immediately checked out of the unit where I was assigned in Maine and started the enroute training required for all prospective squadron executive officers.

My family and I arrived in Guam on Friday, July 17, 1981. The very next day, I was on the base and in the executive officer's office of my new squadron. A commander was acting as the squadron executive officer, and I can't say we hit it off right away. But I was all over the squadron that day and the next, and I quickly developed a sense of what wasn't "right" with the unit. First of all, it was huge. There were almost 900 people deployed all over the western Pacific and Indian Ocean that included a permanent detachment in Japan and a semi-permanent one in the Philippines. I was coming from an assignment as officer in charge of a unit of just 18 officers and 90 enlisted troops where I knew everyone and everyone knew me. Second, I was being given every nitpicking little problem to solve, and few if any of my squadron officers were taking the initiative required to do their jobs. They were used to taking all of their problems to the commanding officer.

I quickly decided that I needed someone who could take care of the myriad of small details any unit could have, which could detract badly from the time I had each day to take care of the big issues. I asked two people if they could recommend someone, preferably a chief petty officer or higher, who might have the flexibility and sense of self to fill my requirements. Both of the men told me about Chief Aviation Electronics Technician Dennis Stager—and it was suggested that he might be the person I was looking for to help me get a handle on the squadron.

Dennis beautifully describes our first encounter in the Introduction, and one of the first things that impressed me about Chief Stager was that he seemed completely at ease and not at all worried about being summoned to see the new executive officer. I spent some time telling Chief Stager about my first

Far Better Shape: Navy Captain Ivan E. Hughes (Ret.)

impressions of the squadron, and to my surprise, he agreed with almost everything I said. I told him that it was my experience that no one on the face of the earth could work harder and do less than a really angry sailor who didn't know why he had to work so hard, didn't feel a part of the unit, and who had little loyalty to that unit. I explained, in some general terms, what I was looking for from him.

That marked the beginning of a relationship and cooperative effort that made VQ-1 into a unit that cared for its people, helped them learn their way in the Navy, and in all honesty, made them into better citizens. Throughout the next 17 months I served as executive officer and an additional 15 months as commanding officer, Chief Stager and I tackled many problems both small and large, and we made VQ-1 into a first-class organization. Essential to this effort was the weeklong "Welcome Aboard" class for all newly reporting enlisted personnel where they were instructed about everything that was expected of them and how to handle living in the unit—including the principles shared in *Surviving Your Feelings*. In addition to the fine work Chief Stager did to help our sailors, I know for sure that his bride, Virginia, had a hand in all the success stories as well.

It was very hard to turn the squadron over to my relief on March 26, 1984, but that is the way it works in naval aviation! In every assignment of my career, I tried to leave the job in better shape than it was when I took over. I can absolutely say that VQ-1 was a far better squadron than it was when I got there in 1981, but I am not so conceited to think that I did it all by myself. Chief Dennis C. Stager was my strong right arm throughout my tour as commanding officer, and I absolutely know in my brain and in my heart that my success came largely through his advice, assistance, and friendship.

As you read and apply *Surviving Your Feelings*, I am convinced Dennis will become your strong right arm, too, as you recognize and deal with your feelings and put your life in far better shape than it may be right now.

BRAVO ZULU!

This is a military statement that means "job well done." It is displayed when you run two different letter flags up the mast to be seen from one ship to another.

Far Better Shape: Navy Captain Ivan E. Hughes (Ret.)

The B [BRAVO] flag is on top, and it is red with the triangle removed from the outer edge, or fly edge, of the flag. The Z [ZULU] flag is flown under it, and it has four triangles with the apexes meeting in the center. Black is on the left next to the line (rope), blue is on the right on the flying side, red is at the bottom, and yellow is at the top.

Introduction

Surviving the Battle with Emotions

Losing this battle will always cause failures in crucial areas of your life.

Fact: People who fail in life have seldom utilized their thoughts to manage their behaviors but are driven by their emotions. Successful people always use thoughts to govern themselves. Observations and origins about validating your thinking skills, testing your values, and putting them in motion are ahead in

Surviving Your Feelings

Surviving Your Feelings. All of the information I will share has been *tested* against historically proven truths and values and proven to me by 29 years in the United States Navy and through reading history.

While I was active in the Navy, the newly arrived executive officer, Navy Commander Ivan E. Hughes, gave me a task during our first meeting. He was about to speak to the chiefs, and I saw him in the passageway of the hangar after his arrival. I was walking toward my workspace, and he approached me on his way to a meeting room. He spotted my name tag and looked me straight in the eye.

"Hello, Chief Stager. I am the new XO. Please come see me Monday, as I want to introduce you to your new job."

"Yes, sir!" I replied respectfully and unafraid. I was an upfront, direct, and often blunt person. I didn't snap to attention or salute. Generally, one doesn't salute an officer inside a building unless coming to a commanding officer's office for the first time. "I start Monday in my new job coordinating the electronic vans."

"No," he said, "I have a different new job for you."

I didn't expect that. "Sir, do you have time to tell me what this new job is, please?"

Introduction: Surviving the Battle with Emotions

He gave a respectful nod and an impressive, non-threatening smile. "Yes, Chief. Very briefly, I want you to clean up this command."

I was flabbergasted. "You want me to clean up this command?" I repeated. The *command* was a 900-plus person command deployed all over the western Pacific.

Inside my head, I was laughing. On the outside, I was obviously puzzled. *He wants me, a tired old chief petty officer nearing retirement, an electronics technician, to be assigned to what is a people person's, impossible-to-do task?*

I shook my head "no"—but his eyes told me he was absolutely serious!

"What is the goal of this cleanup?" I queried.

"A 180-degree turnaround," he replied.

I had been there long enough to admit that there were many things that needed to be addressed. The specific problems do not need to be described here, but they were evident, and I was aware of them.

Then the executive officer clarified, "You're going to be my new human resources officer."

That was a position usually held by a senior Naval officer.

"Sir, I don't want this new job," I stated boldly. Being *only* a Chief Petty Officer E-7 versus an O4-5 Naval Officer, I knew my rank, position, and previous responsibilities.

He replied softly but with unmistakable emphasis, "Chief, you've got the job."

Since it was clear he was as serious as a heart attack, I simply had to ask, "How am I supposed to do this clean up?"

His answer threw me for a loop.

"I don't know, but you can do it!"

"*Yes*, sir," I stated, "but what will be my license?" I was curious just how far my authority and influence would reach.

"I don't know, specifically," he answered. "Whatever it takes."

Another loop! "That," I paused, "is a lot of rope, sir."

With a sly grin, he looked me straight in the eyes. "Yes, it is!"

"Well, sir," I continued, "How will I know when I have reached the end of my new rope?"

"I will tap on it," he replied. To tap on the line is old school, hard hat, Navy deep water diver lingo.

Introduction: Surviving the Battle with Emotions

Differing taps convey information to the diver while underwater. His reply and the direct approach it conveyed triggered my next question.

"How do I know you won't hang me with this new rope, sir?"

He leaned in and spoke softly but, again, most emphatically.

"Chief, I *know* who *you* are! Now *you* need to find out who *I* am."

Then I replied, most respectfully, "Aye, Aye, sir!"

Remember, we had only met four minutes earlier—but there was certainly no doubt in my mind that he was *real!*

Based on some of my most recent past experiences and observations, that exchange was *very* refreshing.

He nodded his head. "See me Monday ten-ish," and he walked away to his meeting.

THE NEW JOB

In minutes, I had lost my job as an electronics technician and been given the impossible job (for me) of being a "people person." I made a few phone calls and found out the new executive officer *could* be trusted

100 percent. In the days that followed, he and I commiserated much and chased around ideas for defined problems, looked for solutions, and set goals. How was I to reach everybody in the command—deployed and local, senior and junior, officers and enlisted—and ultimately end up with a smoothly working, mission successful, professional command?

I had been given a lot of new jobs in my career, but this one was frightening at that stage. I knew little about human resources.

Again, I wondered, *Can I, a technician, be a people person?*

THE TOOL HUNT

Many people were asked this question: "What is the universal foundational item for successful leadership, melded with enjoyable, trusting followership?" Several responses identified the who, where, and why, but none answered the what and how.

Then, one day I visited Chief Frank, the director of the local command's drug and alcohol recovery program to pick his brain. On our way back to his office after getting a cup of coffee together, we walked

Introduction: Surviving the Battle with Emotions

by the partially open door to a classroom for a drug and alcohol recovery group. A black and white film was being shown of a presentation by Father Martin, a renowned civilian counselor in the drug and alcohol recovery field.

In it, he was writing on a chalkboard a list of emotions that get us into trouble.

Chapter 1

A Place to Start

On every voyage, raise the anchor, add power, and steer to the destination.

Wham! Emotions started flashing in my mind. They are the cornerstone of *everyone's* world, and I realized they would be the keystone to growing our leadership program.

I gulped my coffee, thanked Chief Frank for what I had just observed with him, and almost ran back to my office. I knew I had found my answer. I quickly drew a rough outline for "Surviving Your

Feelings," remembering three vital side notes to guide my engagement.

Cannot Preach.

Cannot Teach.

Must Reach!

After many years of teaching technical stuff, I knew that the only way to reach any diverse population was to use *their* knowledge, not mine.

I was then, and still am today, unable to present a single approach to this most complex subject that succeeds in everybody understanding and taking responsibility for these sensitive ideas and truths.

LESSON FROM HISTORY

An old adage states that people only learn what they *want* to learn and what they think they *need* to learn. Most importantly, they're best taught what they learn for themselves.

We can call that "experience."

How do we get experience in a classroom? The answer is mathematical. For example, if there are 35 people in a room whose average age is 25, then 25 x 35 = 875 years of experience. Being 44 years of age at that time, their combined experience ratio was 19-to-1 better than my own.

Who can compete with that?

SOCRATIC METHOD OF TEACHING

I knew of only one way to tap that experience, and that was to ask questions, but there was no need to get too personal. A useful and successful question was, "Can you give an example of a nasty emotion?" They didn't have to reveal their own nasty emotion, but one in general. Who wants to admit nasty thoughts and emotions from their own history.

Emotions are seldom a coffee table discussion subject. People are often told to "compartmentalize" them or told, "You shouldn't feel that way."

We must, however, learn to live with them successfully.

WHY?

Asking non-invasive questions allowed everyone present to give examples of positive and negative emotions. Our discussions also involved the "triggers" that drove those emotions to the surface.

This universally applicable presentation, "Surviving

Surviving Your Feelings

Your Feelings," was first used as the introduction for a three-day Leadership and Welcome Aboard Seminar. Steadily over the next 18 months, I facilitated this discussion to everybody in the command from commanding officer on down. No one was left out. At the end of those 18 months, people started coming in from other commands to see what we were doing, ready to hear the information I was presenting. The widely deployed command I taught experienced several positive changes as a result of those 18 months-plus of training.

- Leadership was achieved, and it was evident to all commandwide and beyond.
- Drug and alcohol abuse became the lowest on record. The recovery success rate was 94 percent with the lowest DWI rate ever. The drug abuse rate was close to zero.
- Re-enlistment rates were the highest ever recorded for that command.
- Aircraft maintenance work time was reduced dramatically from six 12 hour shifts a week down to four 10 hour shifts a week.
- Quality control by all hands became extremely good.

A Place to Start

- Completed mission assignments improved by nearly 45 percent.
- Marriage problems were dramatically reduced.
- The discipline needed from top command was virtually nil.
- Problems were solved at lower leadership levels.
- Morale was very high.

Command improvements were so apparent that a senior naval officer visited from a more senior naval command wanting to know specifically what we were doing to create the success.

BOTTOM LINE

Standard leadership responsibility training to successfully deal with emotions increased the energy and willingness of the command to perform at peak levels at all stages. Personal accountability thrived.

This approach to a very vital and, sadly, ignored part of our lives proved to be very effective. This foundational technique, openly discussed, created belonging, solid self-identity, plus…

The freedom to live responsible lives.

Surviving Your Feelings

Lives free of drugs, alcohol, and the things we use to stay busy so we do not "think of the stuff."

What follows has been tested. It's not rocket science, there are no special theorems, and no doctorate is needed to facilitate this growth in your life. Senior and junior military personnel, civilians, Ph.Ds., college students, high school dropouts, and grade school children can *all* find the freedom to become responsible, upright, and trustworthy people. Then the "Oh, you poor baby" concept is left behind in the dust. Reality rules.

Chapter 2

Nah, Don't Take My Word for It. Test "It."

**All valid truth can be tested and
seen to have zero faults.**

In the 20-plus years after attending my seminar, people have come to me and said, "It saved my life. I am successful."

But it was not because of me. "It" was learning to handle their own emotions. My best advice is to test "it" by studying a balanced account of truly successful people throughout history. You will find that all those who calmly dealt with themselves and their emotions are considerate and use reality, candor, and openness to let people in.

One bad technique to recognize that you should never use when handling emotions is to scream at others, hollering wide eyed, calling names, slobbering, spitting, or making faces behind someone's back. The goal of those who regularly use screaming as a technique is control. They are often attempting to forcefully convince others to get in line and on board to comply and become part of the "team" simply because they say so. They'll declare statements such as, "I am right!" or "Everybody knows it's constitutional!" We see such emotional confabulation in many places.

Yes, of course, emotions are real, but they don't always reflect reality. Overly emotional people can change in microseconds. Reality rarely changes that fast. That's why a valid technique in dealing with your emotions is to seek reality and truths based on historically proven values. Values that have been presented in many ways as tools for life that do no harm. They leave no need to compromise or avoid. They require no sugar coating, no flashy disguise, and no lies to remember.

There are many examples of historically proven values. The "Soul Maintenance Handbook" (my name for the Bible) is one universal book that historically provides clues to finding successful results in life. The New Life Version[1] is the most direct and simple version of this "handbook" that will reveal values that work if they are used.

FOUNDATIONAL TRUTHS

To successfully survive your feelings, avoid ideas that are not truths. Such untruths have no direction point to assist you in detecting tested, productive pathways to dealing with your emotions. They are false tracks that do not guide you on a path of responsible freedom but, instead, lead you down deep, licentious ditches of doctrine that give power to the slicksters and screamers. Valid truths will always be consistently solid and do no harm as guidance.

LEARN TO DEAL WITH THE "STUFF"

When it's all said and done, you will be able to empty

Surviving Your Feelings

your garbage bucket of negative emotions and put your solid, enjoyable feelings, truths, and honorable memories—your "cookies"—in your new, cleaned up, and polished cookie jar! This different approach to a cleaner life will open doors and provide bridges formally unavailable and often unseen by you.

One caution: you must rinse the bucket, meaning that you need to identify all negative and destructive emotions, along with the triggers that initiate them, then relegate the negatives to yesterday. Tell them, "Not me. Not here. Not now." Remember, you cannot carry yesterday.

The clean-up will result in success moving upon clear paths for you and leadership for others.

Notes

1. New Life Version of the Holy Bible, Copyright 1969-2003, Christian Literature, P.O Box 777, Canby, Oregon 97013. Now published by Barbour Publishing, Inc.

Chapter 3

Surviving "Your" Feelings

**Only after surviving your feelings
can you walk tall and free.**

Feelings and emotions are a truth in life. In my many years of study and counseling, I have yet to meet anyone who is, in fact, without emotions. It goes without saying that some people who have extreme mental troubles will often not display emotions or try to act as though they never even had emotions, but time will prove they are just like everyone else. So, to be historically factual, everyone has emotions.

Surviving Your Feelings

No one jumps off a bridge based on a rational truth. No one drives into a tree or a crowd of people with truth as their guide. No one murders, rapes, steals, or does anything wrong against others or themselves using truthful thought to trigger those behaviors.

Only *your* emotions can initiate you to a wrongful cycle.

Very few of us will start screaming and dumping our perceived mistreatments on someone who is not close to us. We normally do this only to those who are seen as safe enough to hear and receive it; specifically, those we trust will not hurt us in return. Likewise, we seldom snarl and let loose our vindictiveness on those whose repercussions we fear. Nevertheless, the provocation is often so emotional we seem to be outside ourselves.

The next day, we may behave like the blowup never happened, bouncing around like life was wonderful. We'll act like a completely different person. But if we're confronted about the emotional dump, we often deny or justify our behavior by blaming others for it to deny our own culpability.

Why are we doing so well the next day? Because we reduced the garbage level in our emotional bucket.

Surviving "Your" Feelings

Lowering the level of our emotional bucket makes life feel better. After all, high levels of garbage are painful to look at and heavy to carry.

WHY DOES THIS HAPPEN?

In truth, each one of us is living life the best we know how with the tools we have at our disposal. This "life toolbox" consists of the actions, behaviors, and expressions we use to solve problems to hopefully produce pleasurable results.

Chapter 4

Using Skill to Build a New Toolbox

Beautiful skills are useless without energy to apply them.

When we grab a tool to address a problem, we often find that the tool is wrong for the task. Maybe it is tainted with anger, fear, hate, or jealousy. Still, we may use it anyway because it is the only tool we have for that job.

We can seldom walk away from a problem that is

having a negative effect on our lives. Yet if, for example, we use the tool of blaming others so we can feel that something is okay—it still won't change our behavior or thought patterns. If our tool is to walk away, denial will still be there to remind us of our failures and faults.

The definition of a broken life tool is an emotionally triggered action or thought that wrongly influences us and misdirects something or someone around us, most often producing wrong results.

How do we get around this problem?

First, recognize the fact that we are honestly doing the best we know how to do. We've *learned* to choose or use the wrong life tools from others. We are all bombarded by people who work full time to convince us they are right and we are wrong. Remember, too, that making a mistake is *not* the same as being wrong. A mistake is *doing* wrong. Doing wrong is an *action*, but being wrong is an *identity*. If our identity is wrong, nearly every action we do will be negative and destructive. Likewise, disagreeing with someone and respectfully asking questions does not make you wrong! We may do wrong in different ways, but that

Using Skill to Build a New Toolbox

only makes our path rougher and leaves us tired. It does not change our identity the way being wrong does.

Second, look at how history provides lessons on how to solve life's problems. The truths of history facilitate a foundational thought process that will guide our actions around to reality. True fact foundations exist to provide the skills we need to build and utilize a new life toolbox.

A thought to consider is this: negatives that you have collected through the years will override and hide the many positive possibilities in your life by battering your thoughts and giving you a negative mindset. These negatives (trash) can make you feel like a total failure and less than everyone else who appears to be "fine." They aren't "fine." They may say they are when asked how they are doing, but deep down they have their own buckets of stinking garbage filled with pain that prevent them from seeing even a small particle of beauty in themselves or life around them. A mind tuned to the negative cannot easily receive positive truths.

Our Designer does not make trash! Bring the negatives to light. Measure them with the white light of truth, and your true values will soon appear.

Chapter 5

Results of Using Tested Life Tools

Using *tested* life tools enables high-quality finished products.

The collected observations expressed in *Surviving Your Feelings* came from hundreds of facilitated discussions with people from all walks of life about that often-ignored, mostly denied, and generally feared subject of conversation—emotions, feelings, impulses. They affect everyone: male and female, old or young, educated or uneducated, from every social, political, military or civilian status. In other words—we the people! All of us carry the potential for the same nasty or cruel feelings. We may have different triggers and varying intensities of energy used up by those triggers, but humans are capable of nearly any emotion we can name.

So, choosing and using tested life tools results in responses that trigger productive behaviors with values that are historically proven to be true, respected, upright, and pure. These values can be loved and are well thought of, good and worthy, do no harm, and make us very thankful.

Thinking with this baseline of values will produce a self that is no longer starving for peace of mind and can experience the next truly visible result: freedom. Freedom from the emotional trash all of us collect but usually do not deal with. Our results at work improve, alcohol and drug abuse are reduced to nearly zero, and social relationships grow stronger with many highly valued friendships gained. After all, though, before we can safely look into the eyes of

Results of Using Tested Life Tools

other people, we must look into our own eyes with true respect and self-worth.

Most of all, we must take charge of our own emotions. They are an inescapable part of everyone's life. They may be subject to constant denial or overshadowed and covered by frantic activity. We can easily fill each day with demands to be or do _____. Then we'll say, "Gotta go! See ya at happy hour!" Why? "Happy hour" presents another excuse to consume substances that ease the mind, numb the fear, and mask the anxiety. It's a time to forget. Many people find themselves absolutely unable to *not* be busy, staying constantly occupied in order to *not* think about anything that demands time, energy, attention, or approval to deal with.

Using tested life tools removes your need for a "happy hour" because you are equipped to deal with your emotions successfully through productive behaviors with values that bring positive results.

Chapter 6

The Monster "It"

Everything has at least two sides. Choose wisely.

Many people chase after the perfect rainbow or long to find that magic person, important job, wonderful place, or special relationship that will allow them to always be happy. The monster "it" is anything that occupies your mind so strongly that everything is influenced by "it" to the point that you'll do anything and everything not to think about "it."

We expend a huge amount of energy to ignore or

avoid the "it" because "it" often brings up strong, pervasive emotions. Even though it may appear we're not at fault for it happening, our negative emotions will only drive us to chase the monkey around the proverbial bush. Emotions, recognized as being transient, can create an awareness of many facets of life, but if they are not controlled by valid thought, they will leave us out of control and not in charge of ourselves. This leaves us racing down a crooked pathway in life toward dangers that are not often apparent but are definitely ahead.

Emotions quite often trigger strong mind activity that we misconstrue to be rational thought, but they are actually false thoughts that regularly and irrationally initiate invalid actions. Valid thoughts based on truth and values are always the same every day. At first glance, many things will look attractive. They'll sound good. After testing and selecting, you can avoid self-destruction.

Therefore, true happiness will never be found until our emotions are no longer in charge. Truths, and a tested set of values guided by a mind that works, are the foundation of success. We become responsible for our happiness only when we take charge of our emotional triggers and defeat the monster "it" for good!

Chapter 7

Life's Lie

**There are very few people who
will not try to dilute truth.**

Often, an emotion driven idea will circle around and around in our minds demanding constant action. Its nagging never lets up, and this can be quite frustrating and even painful. We may hide, deny, run away, and paint over this idea in any way we can to try to justify it. We may also make a blind call and attempt to relabel it, claiming it is a strength or something we deserve or have earned.

Surviving Your Feelings

The latest social or political sayings will sometimes attempt to justify their ideas. The slogans "Black Lives Matter" and "Make America Great Again" are both sayings that people respond to according to their personal social and political views. When we subscribe to one of these sayings, we then belong to that group of people. We are likely to march to the tune of their pipers and feel like one of the atta-boys or atta-girls of the collective. Masking up and disappearing in a screaming crowd is not belonging!

Then, because the leaders of those groups declared that only what we believe as this collective is important, it suddenly gives *you* the right to do whatever pops into their minds to accomplish, even if it is destructive or hurts other people. Your responsibility for such actions is thrown out the window. How you *feel* becomes the only thing that matters.

Yet such ideas are seldom based fully on historical, tested truth. Platitudes, even ones that are frequently used, never become truthful in and of themselves. They merely make us appear to belong. Spouting these ideas is usually accompanied by childish faces made behind someone's back, finger waving, or wide-eyed

Life's Lie

accusations toward those with whom we disagree. We may even choose to ignore those people altogether.

The declaration, "That is how I feel!" is life's lie—and it is often used as an excuse for responding to an emotional trigger. But behaving according to your feelings is rarely successful, except for maybe choosing a cereal for breakfast. Using emotions alone, people hurry through life trying to keep ahead of the monsters in and of the dark.

Emotions can shift many times in a matter of seconds. Fact-triggered actions seldom shift except within the few variables. For example, a fact-triggered action to drive from Point A to Point B would be to get in your car, turn on the ignition, and proceed. Variables of whether you go fast or slow down the road come into play, but those variables don't change the fact-triggered action or turn it into a lie. Emotions can also trigger different actions, but facts and truth trigger *correct* actions.

Awareness of this will help you get in the driver's seat and speed up or slow down to take control of your life a bit at a time. Don't expect everything to change immediately. Take small bites. Recognize your emotions and triggers, and you will bring an end to those nagging ideas.

Chapter 8

The Upward Ladder

Each step higher brings more light. Scary or thrilling, it depends upon *your* ladder.

The darkness of a life kept in a prison of flooding emotions is frightful. Even naming individual emotions can be difficult at times because they are a heavy part of our history. Anxiety, fear, guilt, and other emotions can initiate other feelings that are hard to grab ahold of and own. Yet once they are out of the dark, they project a smaller, less frightening shadow.

Surviving Your Feelings

It is an upward ladder, one not easily climbed, but as you name it, claim it, own it, and deal with it, the light of guidance based on truth will arrive a patch at a time. When tested, valid truth illuminates the subject, and problems shrink into manageable bits. Then, once you are on the ladder, you have a choice to either go up or down. Nobody can stand on a ladder and not take a step one way or the other. A bird never lands on a limb and stays there its whole life.

Look *around* you and watch the behavior patterns of others who claim to be fine but in reality are being chased by the demons of the dark. They seek emotional anesthetics, commonly used substances such as drugs and alcohol, to numb nagging emotions, persistent feelings of failure, and the guilt reminder bugs collected in their emotional bucket. This causes the "haunted" look we often see in people's eyes.

Then look *within* yourself—and allow the emotional fragility you see in others to make you aware of the changes you need to make so that you can build a foundational mindset of choosing and using positive life tools to identify solid paths in life. Awareness of other's emotions will also help you realize that you are not alone and reinforce your sense of belonging. Remember, though, that not everyone reaches the same level of awareness at the same time.

That's why the facilitated discussion of *Surviving Your Feelings* in a group setting is so successful and strengthening. It gives a valuable lesson in belonging. We all have emotions, and all of us can survive them. Dealing with our emotions is better than running from them.

Chapter 9

Running From Life's Little Demons

When fleeing from them, glancing back wastes precious energy.

"Happy hour" finds people racing to the bar to get away from the load of life and experience in an attempt to find a temporary, short, numbing respite from the garbage life often presents and the pain that garbage brings.

It's an age-old phenomenon that reminds us about

the long race we run, hurrying to leave the demons behind and arrive at happiness on time. We speed through the first drink. Why? The common answer I often heard is, "A drink or two helps me to be sociable and ready for 'happy hour.'"

Alcohol, the emotional anesthetic, may be the fastest route to "happy hour." It reduces thinking capacity and clouds the mind. For a while, at least, it seems to even take away the pain. But it's also a costly one. According to www.bw166.com, a company that provides advisory and data science services to alcohol beverage retailers, over $398 billion was spent on consumable alcohol in the United States in the 12 months before September 2023 alone.

Alcohol use is also the main social tool that derails our trains of thought with "facts" or "truths" that may not be validatable so that we may rationalize our behavior, justify our emotions, and act upon them without immediate guilt or shame. This then facilitates the shifting of our own errors to something or someone else outside of ourselves. After they have been caught doing something wrong, people often say, "Well, I was drunk or high," or "They hurt my feelings," or "It felt right at the time." In those cases, our emotions drive our mind with no reflection or direction from reality or truth.

During a conversation among old friends, someone remembered and declared, "Ordinary is the man or woman who will enjoy the fruits of one glass of wine, but rare are those who can resist the second glass. Too often, we glimpse the wreckage of those who cannot count nor break the chains that bind them."

(This is not my statement, but its wisdom is clear.)

Another factor that doesn't help matters is news headlines and social media posts that hammer us with their bleating messages of "legality" regarding the "right" of people to use drugs, or advertisers that constantly promote drugs or various organic compounds that will make you feel better, despite their side effects. It seems there is a pill for everything. Just be sure to consult with your doctor.

Alcohol and drugs create various sensations that temporarily cause feelings of euphoria or numbing that appear to chase the demons back into the dark. Of course, no one uses alcohol or drugs to feel bad or worse. Yet I believe a truly effective "war" on drugs should focus more on a crusade to teach emotional control in life *without* any chemicals. Lives will *blossom* and freedom from addiction *will* come, closing its costly and often deadly detours that manipulate our minds toward rationalizing our behavior and leading away from worthwhile goals just so we can temporarily "feel" better.

Sadly, teaching youngsters about drugs and their various effects on the user over the past five decades may have actually contributed to the massive increase in drug abuse during that same time period. Why? Conflicting messages. On one hand, we tell them drugs can be harmful. On the other hand, we declare that to be happy in life, "Just do it!" So, when certain drugs are legalized by dubbing them to be recreational or medicinal, that sound advice and rational thinking that says drug abuse is not okay is tossed aside by our perceived "right" to have and use these drugs as much as we want.

Our rights? What about our responsibilities, including all of their costs?

We have abandoned rational thinking, substituting it with emotional pleas for our rights. This has driven many people into the darkness of untruths, lies that cry out, "To each his own!" "Different strokes for different folks!" Since we are all different and unique, each of us can do as we please. Never mind the consequences to ourselves or others. If we *each* have our own standards and values, how is it possible to have a sense of community?

People have told me, "You don't know how I feel," which, of course, instantly closes the door to normal conversation. No wonder we routinely see groups of individuals sitting at a dinner table, each person tapping on their little colored boxes with bright lights and noises emitting from them, seemingly "communicating" in code to others so that no one can understand what is being implied, much less said. It's just more of "to each his own" fitted with the tired, old shoe of "rights." The holes that allow constant bumps to reach our soles do get bigger and make those shoes worrisome and often painful indeed.

Rational thought is left in the dust and trash of a hurtful life, resulting in failing behavior patterns that feed the narrative of failed actions—actions often justified by being drunk or under the influence of drugs.

Surviving Your Feelings

These failed actions, in truth, are best expressed as "non-thinking activity"—and life's little demons, far from vanquished, keep coming back for more.

The old adage is true. "Anyone can make a fool out of themselves, but they have to be stupid to stay there."

Chapter 10

Life's Bucket of Pain

Why continue carrying a bucket filled with pain-inducing chunks?

After someone commits a serious, erroneous action, you may hear the perpetrator's neighbors swear that they would never have thought that person even remotely capable of considering or doing such a stupid, terrible thing. Obviously, he or she was a nice, quiet, thoughtful person, always busy helping others, driving their immaculate, vintage street rod quietly because they are so shy and considerate. "Who would have thought they would steer it into a crowd while screaming, ranting, and raving? They must have been drugged or something!"

No—they were in pain, and the fear of more pain blew their emotional bucket apart.

As I stated earlier in *Surviving Your Feelings*, many emotions are painful and even shameful. They can come from many aspects of life, and they are not all of our intentional making. Yet these emotions are *ours*. Anyone is capable of every emotion describable, triggered by thoughts, memories, words and actions of others, or situations that are fearful. Ugly words, failures, and guilt from some dark hole in a person's history can collect and concentrate the anxieties and stresses, resulting in more pain.

Also, as mentioned before, we do not like to recognize these emotions, so we do many things to avoid feeling them or even admitting that we have them. All the while, they accumulate in the recesses of our emotional bucket. When triggered, they come to the forefront. When they rise to the surface, we can no longer deny them or cover them up with booze, drugs, food, sex, or fast cars. Those emotions take

Life's Bucket of Pain

charge of our thoughts. We only see a life with more pain on the horizon. Good cannot be recognized anywhere. It is filtered out by the mud of pain.

This frightens us. Our rational thinking is overridden—and murder and suicide often happen to stop this cycle.

Sadly, the stimulation we feel from the anticipation of pleasure can also drive us to the brink. When the good stuff is used up, its memory isn't vivid enough to stave off the pain. We simply seek more pleasure to avoid the parts of life that we cannot handle. Yet the bad stuff continues to accumulate and rot, becoming a reeking lump of fear and pain. Such denial also slams the door to solving the problems or managing the triggers that fire up our emotions. It gathers, festers, and turns into a waiting dragon with scary, fiery breath—then the negative emotions blow up explosively at the strangest of times and most unlikely of places.

We may tell our boss or co-worker bad thoughts about them that we had stored up for years.

Bad events remain as reminders of past pain, and we recall and recite previous hurts like they happened two minutes ago.

Surviving Your Feelings

We scream, attack, and throw stuff.

We smash priceless items because they are connected to a person we blame for an anxious or fearful emotion.

Many times, and more often than not, we blow up at loved ones or people we have known and treasured for years. Why? They are safe. Then, an hour later, we will appear to not realize how our outburst happened in the first place. This is often how it is for those who abuse others. They'll apologize and promise it will *never* happen again, and maybe it won't—until the next infusion of alcohol or drugs, and then the cycle starts all over again.

Why do we seldom, if ever, blow up at someone who is not "safe?" They might hurt us, whereas we don't fear our safe relationships will attack us in retribution. Usually, only they see the explosions that result from our accumulation of emotional garbage. Our collection of pain, guilt, and fear ensures there is no end to the stuff.

Haven't you had your fill of it? Pain in excess takes a lot of energy and intense concentration to carry and conceal. Pain so intense it's absolutely terrifying

Life's Bucket of Pain

to know that more is coming, and that only amplifies the pain. It becomes a horror more fearful to face than death itself. Heavy and burdensome is a bucket of nasties, often creating pain beyond tolerable limitations.

It's our bucket, however.

Is that *truly* the reality?

No. But it sure feels terrible.

Last thought: It's our bucket, but we must deal with it along the path to freedom.

Chapter 11

The Emotional Bucket

Why do we carry pain filled buckets? They're our buckets!

When you think of life's bucket of pain, picture it as a steel-ribbed garbage can topped by a strong lid with locks and valves. It's a strange apparatus, but it is specially designed to store and hide fearful and hurtful emotions. The lid has a name on it.

Denial.

The lid is there to keep unwanted, monstrous,

Surviving Your Feelings

nasty feelings out of our thoughts and away from triggering wrong behaviors. The locks and valves secure the cargo and release the pressure as needed to keep it from blowing off as we shove more and more pain into it. Emotions of this caliber elicit constant reminders of our failures, guilt, and shame, so the container is ceaselessly pressurized with more and more emotions that we are unwilling to recognize and deal with.

However, when the valves crack and the locks break, the lid shoots off into the air, and the emotions swirl out like a vicious black tornado. Terrible actions take place, as have been described previously. You can easily identify and define your own explosive list, as well as those you've seen in others. The destruction is often fierce and total.

Again, I will remind you: name it, claim it, own it, and deal with it.

One effective way to help deal with our emotions is to talk about them with someone we trust. *Confession* has been used for years to assist folks in reducing the garbage in their emotional bucket. Sadly, various techniques have been used to control people as they

The Emotional Bucket

fall into a mechanical system of repeated confessions that allow for a constant repetition of failures that creates a cycle that prevents us from dealing with the emotions. Confession should never be used as an excuse for future destructive choices.

One nearly universal tool to apply is to "talk not walk." Walking away from problems only allows the pressure to build so that the eventual explosion of emotions is even greater than first imagined. Talking, however, works because it is a way to truthfully *do* something about the garbage.

For example, have you ever sat beside someone on a plane as they told you stuff about their lives that they would never tell anybody else? Yet when the plane lands they smile and say, "Thanks, it was nice talking with you," then leave the aircraft tall and upright. Why? Because they will *never* see you again. You were safe. They have a grin on their face and a bounce in their step because the level of garbage is lower in their emotional bucket. The pressure is less because they gave it to you by talking instead of walking away.

Speaking about the garbage in your emotional

Surviving Your Feelings

bucket is healthy. Denying it and choosing to stay mired in the mistakes of your past is not. Here is what I've learned about the past. Yesterday is a word to describe a place for lost dreams, regrets for wasted time, shame for shame itself, guilt for deeds done or not done, fears that might find out, shreds of hope that fall apart, and many emotional connections that have been turned into a fearful mass that we would sell for a bent penny.

The truth is, yesterday is gone. You cannot reach it, so consider unloading it by dealing with the negative emotions it creates. Name them so the truth can find and replace them. Bring them into the light with valid hope, look for any key value that remains, and use the lessons you discover. Try to never look back. Your goal is in front of you in your dreams and in your clean heart.

Chapter 12

All of Us Deal with "It"

**Hiding "It" does not prevent it
from growling in the dark.**

Dealing with "It" is healthy. Name it, claim it, own it, and deal with it by working to dump it and never denying it. Before we can handle anything, we must identify it.

The "Soul Maintenance Handbook" has a line that says, "Seek a trusted friend and confess your sins to one another." Yet we should be our *own* best friend. This requires us to first and foremost trust ourselves.

Surviving Your Feelings

Everybody has an idea what "sin" is, but here is another definition. Sin is **S**trongly **I**nitiated **N**efarious behavior. It is always an action that hurts you or someone else.

Sin or bad behavior does harm, the nasty garbage thoughts it generates does harm, and harm is wrong. When we are fortunate enough to have a trusted friend, they can know our faults and failures without rubbing our nose in the garbage. They can also know the pain, stress, fear of being caught, and other consequences of bad behavior.

That's good. But can we trust ourselves with "it" all?

No, so we stay busy, unable to look people in the eye because it feels like they know what we are doing or see the stuff we are carrying. Our casual friends will never hear us talk of the painful junk that has accumulated. Why would they? When asked, "How are you doing?" they are the ones who give the common answer, "Oh, fine." Really? So, since everyone we know looks fine and says they're fine, we must be the one with the problem!

Tell someone? Not on your life.

Why?

All of Us Deal with "It"

Rejection.

Rejection is hard enough without having someone else see what we "feel," way down deep in the cesspool of our emotional bucket. To be rejected by them after seeing the rotten stuff in there is unthinkable.

However, we can do something that is both very helpful and enjoyable—join the family. *Everybody* has an emotional bucket with their own stuff inside. Since that emotional stuff is nasty, most everyone else keeps it quiet to avoid rejection, too. Feelings are always around. They're ours and they're theirs. We all have our own emotions, and we all struggle with them similarly.

Emotions that trigger a behavior we would never admit to doing.

Nasty thoughts that seem to arrive out of the clear blue, and we cannot prove where they come from.

Impulses outside of ourselves that some even call demonic.

We all have that in common.

We also share the ability to employ values and truth to prevent us from following through with horrible actions triggered by nasty emotions. In addition, each of us knows, or can know, the feelings that clue us in that we are about to act in a horrible way.

All of us can deal with "it."

If you do not handle your emotions, they will imprison you. Successful people deal with their emotions. Dealing is not letting your feelings initiate wrongful behaviors. It is using thoughtful thinking to control those emotions and govern those behaviors. Identifying triggers and connecting them to the source of that trigger allows you to take charge of them. Measure your triggers against truth and logical thinking. A thought-driven life brings freedom.

We are all in the same boat. That's why a group approach to *Surviving Your Feelings* was so successful and has helped many hundreds of people to make it through the barrage of emotions we face every moment of every day. Finding the truth that all of us have garbage feelings is a cleansing idea. It lets us know that we are not alone.

Chapter 13

Counter the Emotional Hype

**Look closely, apply the test, keep
the good, and reject the rest.**

*S*urviving Your Feelings facilitates an open discussion that does not invade your private emotional world. Rather, it creates avenues for identifying common yet harmful emotions. This observation allows you to learn the skills required to handle any emotions. Does your "Hunky Dory," your flagship of emotions, have a nasty bilge or leak? It can be repaired with time-tested actions and results-proven truths. These truths provide a base for your thinking, for if you have no foundation, you cannot have a successful life.

Truth prevents us from being emotionally driven people whose identity is sadly revealed as they scream at those they disagree with, ranting, raving, sputtering, and spitting as they accuse others of being wrong. Emotionally driven individuals seldom admit their own actions are wrong. simply accuse others of not understanding and being at fault, as though having different opinion is a major crime. They also often support or turn a blind eye toward socially destructive behaviors. Too many people wrongfully demand others validate their emotionally driven actions.

Many of us want to drive the car of our lives before we know how to steer it. Many want to do this even before we sit down and discuss our lives. We often hear folks say, "*Never* discuss religion or politics." Why do you suppose that is?

Religion, as some people discern it, is a set of absolute values and associated actions that are written in stone. The adherent is correct. All others are wrong. Many who call themselves Christians or Muslim or

Counter the Emotional Hype

Buddhist will not even have lunch with the folks from down the street who believe differently than they do. Why? Those from other sects are labeled, blinded by the mistruths of their belief systems. We can only be what we are, yet once we understand the difference between "being" wrong and "doing" wrong, we realize we can change what we *do,* and that changes what we are *capable* of doing.

Politics is a field where one can gain power and fame. It is very often sought after by people with position-seeking egos who, more often than not, use emotional phrases to incite thoughts in others that create a false sense of belonging and trust. They'll use emotional buzzwords to trigger guilt in other people who they believe have failed or don't have social standing or lots of money. They repeatedly express that only those who support their values are really worthy to understand "truth" while all others are unworthy and deceived in one way or another. These differences are deemed to be licenses to mistreat people. Oftentimes, we hear that the opposite party folks are an enemy to be destroyed.

How can you counter the emotional hype caused

by the religious or political zealots in our lives? First, talk with others. That will close idea gaps and develop a common ground of values where we grow closer and wiser but still disagree.

Second, listen to their speeches and separate the facts from the rhetoric. Sort out those ideas based upon tested truths, not emotional hopes that are often expressed as facts and repeated forcefully until they sound truthful. Some call it *spin*. Identify these mantras and test them.

Third, discern the emotionalism that is the basis for their expressions to find the carrot that's being dangled to the audience. Watch their body actions and match them with the buzz words they use. This will give you more clues to genuine truth than that they professed. Observe how they look at each other. Eye movements will provide insights to the internal workings of their mindset. All of this will help you identify the actual foundation for their expressions and priorities.

Finally, let those observations reveal the motives for their communications. Jumping on a particular bandwagon but ignoring true motives sets you up for

Counter the Emotional Hype

a false sense of belonging where you reject all others, allowing emotions instead of reason to drive your actions. Intensely longing for the warmth of togetherness can actually prevent belonging from growing.

Countering the emotional hype of others is vital because belonging is a common, universal need of people that is greatly desired but seldom found. However, it's when you discover and experience *valid* belonging that the emotional garbage of your life can be dealt with and expelled.

Chapter 14

Belonging

Don't hop on the hype train. Look, think, and *get off* before you get trapped.

After years of questioning people in crisis, I've discovered that they expend much time and energy seeking that most valuable of shelters: a sense of belonging. It is a shelter that makes us feel warm and secure in life, so it is understandable that fear pops its ugly head up whenever our shelter of belonging is cracked and we hear the angry and starving wolves howling outside its walls. Yet our sense of belonging is only valid when the price we pay for it is voluntary, not a forced, harmful, costly fine demanded by the society around us.

Belonging should never be sought after if the price for it requires behaviors that violate proven cornerstones of truth.

The need to belong is expressed by many behaviors that, when looked at logically and truthfully, become whimsical and wasteful. For example, wearing certain clothes and body decorations in order to belong may, in the long run, cost more than what is needed to enjoy genuine belonging. Vulnerable, easily led folks may end up in gangs or become society's puppets as they are fed stuff that creates a sense of belonging without the safety of true friendship. People desperate to belong may end up with their expensive clothes being torn into shredded, clinging rags when they imitate some Hollywood hero or heroine or an aggrandized, self-labeled social group.

Our desire to belong may trigger behaviors that some mimic and follow, telling everyone that we are part of "this" group or "that" species of thought.

Belonging

Nasty and illegal initiation actions to prove gang loyalty destroy many truths.

Unisex make-up with its millions of colors and shades may sparkle, shine, and glow in the dark, but what is the adornment aimed at providing? To whom is it directed?

Faces and bodies with enough metal hanging from them to make a barbed wire fence may attract attention, but to what end? Where do we find the codes that the gadgets convey?

Cartoons and movies whose messages are purported to be real are often just computer-generated animations that express ideas and behaviors most people will not choose to accept until hidden behind closed doors. Whose values do they connect with?

Television shows are touted as family programs yet labeled as PG, but where is the parental guidance? How can you apply guidance after the nasty trash that has already flashed on the screen? Just talk it away? Advertising seeks money to support this or that program or protection while entertainment directors make more money than heads of valid businesses. Who is this aimed at? What hungers do they fulfill?

Surviving Your Feelings

Panhandlers will tell you that the guilt of emotionally fragile people is the most common reason they roll down the windows of their cars and hand them money or pull over to buy them a hamburger. Why do they need to assuage their guilt?

The reason for all of it is that we want to belong.

But we're seeking it all wrong. The price we pay is too high and the reward is too little. The sense of belonging we receive is false and incomplete.

Therefore, turn away from the influences mentioned earlier that try to make you feel like you belong. Many divisions in our society are political and are not based on true values. Parties in power tend to use emotionally driven goals to control people instead of following their oaths to serve. They, in turn, trigger racial fragmentations that rise yet disappear during a crisis or military tasking. Truth takes over and provides the guidance needed to solve the crises tasks. History is replete with examples of successes gained by strangers who came together to solve problems.

Social engineers have convinced many that a young boy or girl can determine their "real" gender identity. Really? What can a child use to make this decision?

Facts? History? Biology? Truth? No. It's determined by how they "feel." How can a boy know how a girl feels? For years, women have been telling grown men they cannot know how a woman feels. So, how can a child know this for certain? Similar social engineering seeks to make everyone seem equal, trustworthy, and part of every solution, yet it fosters only division. The United States of America was founded upon solid, common values that have made it one of the most successful societies in the world. But social splintering in every area of our culture has reduced us to the point where emotions are the most powerful driving force in people's lives.

Emotions can influence what we feel, what we think, and what we do, but negative emotions provide no healing and zero sense of valid belonging.

Social engineering needs to be rejected. Those vying for votes and power through disingenuous promises of equal pay and equal resources need to be ignored. Anything that promotes freedom and rights without individual responsibility needs to be refused.

Why?

Surviving Your Feelings

All of it creates a fake, weak sense of belonging that is, at best, temporary and is always doomed to fail.

True belonging—belonging that will make our nation whole once again—begins one person at a time, starting with you.

Only *you* can deal with your emotions so that genuine belonging can become a constant reality in your life.

Chapter 15

Truth: The Way to True Belonging

Truth is valid on all sides. There is no smoke and mirrors.

Truth shows a set of visible and testable standards of being, looking, and seeing that allows us to have values and genuinely belong with no harm to anyone.

In fact, people who have truth-based values and know how to think ethically are not hooked by the current fad and will never seek out, much less belong to, the "beautiful people crowd." Truth causes them to possess a beauty that is obvious to all. People with truth-based values can look at a situation, test the resources, measure the goals, look for the talent, and make it happen. Then when the job is completed, we all win.

Should everyone who played softball today get a participation trophy designed to keep wrongful emotions out and save the player from being hurt? No. That outcome isn't reality, and it sets the participant, and everyone else, up for a terrible crash and burn scenario with no social engineering proof to support it.

True belonging is glued together by truths and values that remain firm even in the dark times. "We" is one the strongest words in the world.

Moreover, people who are taught to be responsible for their own emotions (i.e., take ownership for their emotions and act accordingly) will apply the historical proof of tested truths and ethical thinking tools to solve problems because they themselves are *free*. Free from all the anchors they dropped into the sticky ocean bottom of garbage that left them stuck by their own emotions, unable to pull up the anchor because its chains were too bound to be released. Free from the substance use that only kept them stuck.

Truth: The Way to True Belonging

Free with no more guilt from the past or fear of the present or of the unknown future.

Those who experience true belonging resulting from their embrace of truth-based values have let go of the garbage of their emotions. Is that garbage gone entirely? No—but they can now handle it when something happens in their lives to trigger it. As they deal with it, one item at a time, it has less and less of an effect on their lives.

I've seen it happen for literally hundreds of people. Garbage gone, that bucket can then become a cookie jar to store memories of life's good emotions and a ready repository of life tools that make and reflect factual and successful behaviors.

There are many ways to teach people these truths in ways where the facilitator will see people change in countenance and composure, sometimes instantly. They can then act with new skills that free them from their negative emotions, as well as find friends who trust each other.

Tested friends are the most valuable treasures in the world.

That is true belonging—and true belonging promotes growth.

Chapter 16

Facilitated Growth

We use GPS to drive vehicles. Using advice from tested sources assists us to live life.

Growth can be facilitated alone or in a discussion. Notes can be taken about anything that comes up and measured against truth to make decisions. The steps that provide the clues to operational truth are 1) look, 2) see, 3) measure against truth, 4) weigh, 5) seek direction, 6) choose applicable skills, and 7) act with your new strengths and 8) enjoy your new position on the ladder toward peace of mind. All of this may require assistance, but the steps and clues provide tangible proof that you are *not* alone in your emotional experiences.

Here is the condensed way this growth occurred in hundreds of groups through my "Surviving Your Feelings" presentations. The Soul Maintenance Handbook tells us to confess our faults to one another. Why? That's the way we find solutions. The human mind seeks answers to most questions that intrigue us or give us light to live by. Many of these questions will only be answered in a safe environment.

In a group setting, questions are used to get the doors open. One I often used is, "Is there anyone here who is *not* human?" That is followed by, "Is there anyone here who does not have feelings or emotions?"

If someone raises their hand or makes a comment stating they don't have emotions, I'll ask, "Do you know what anger or laughter is?" They may nod or say "yes." I'll then reply, "Thanks. From that point of agreement, I'd like us to take a little closer look at examples of things that are often ignored or denied."

As you continue, remember that most people spend an inordinate amount of time and energy

Facilitated Growth

protecting their privacy and their identity. Therefore, try to avoid the impulse to demand that the door be opened should you knock and find that it is not opened right away. That will only shut people down and put them on the defensive. Remember, keep an eye on your own door. You'll never know when an angel may knock.

In many a group, I've then opened the discussion by saying, "I would like to tap the wide experience here to better identify the traps we can encounter in life." This establishes that my knowledge, compared to a room full of people, is naturally limited. We need a large range of responses, and the knowledge they represent, to move forward effectively and, in reality, rapidly.

I then ask, "Would you each please give an example of a nasty emotion in life?" Notice how I presented that query so that the responses are not automatically identified as being *theirs*. That is the beauty of the process. I thankfully take an answer from everyone in the room and write the negative emotions on a board. Next, I draw a depiction of a ribbed bucket with a lid, placing circles around it and labeling those circles (fear, hate, jealousy, etc.) with the triggers that ignite those negative emotions. I usually end up gathering twice the number of emotions than there are people in attendance.

From there, I ask for examples of good emotions from life, and I list them the same way with their own buttons on the bucket circled by triggers. By now, the board should display a wide variety of responses, providing many examples from which we can prove the universality of emotions. You'll discover that many positive emotions and their triggers can be interconnected with negative emotions and triggers.

Then I ask, "Can any of these emotions and triggers be both good and bad?" Frequently, someone will express an idea with anger or forced laughter different from the normal tone of the group. When that happens, simply respond by saying, "Thank you. I have never heard that idea expressed quite that way before." This is a great way to handle an emphatic statement without turning off the person who gave it.

Based on the responses, I'll draw lines connecting those good and bad emotions and triggers. The

Facilitated Growth

group is fully engaged in the discussion and drawn in by the content on the board.

"Now," I say, "Would you please look at the lists on the board. Is there anyone here who has not, at some time, felt every one of those emotions?"

This question is usually met with silence. Sometimes someone in the group may reply "yes." When that occurs, if they volunteer to cite the emotions, I like to respond, "Thank you." Another constructive response at this point is to say, "Please, without saying a word, would everyone look at the person across the table from you, straight in the eyes, and stay silent one full minute." Folks will shuffle and squirm. After all, some have never looked a stranger in the eye in their lifetime, let alone someone they're familiar with.

After the minute is over, softly and with a non-accusing voice, announce, "I want you to know this. All of you are looking at another person who has *the same crappy feelings* you do. All of us share the same emotions and triggers." Then I quickly add, "You're also looking at another person who has all the good stuff you have."

Surviving Your Feelings

It sounds simple, I know—but it is inclusive and powerful.

The door is now fully opened to equip your attendees to begin using their thoughts to manage the behaviors driven by their emotions to govern themselves and proceed toward freedom.

The emotions on the board each have different sensitivity levels. Some require a heavy push to trigger the response. Others are so sensitive that a minor action, word, sound, color, or piece of music will trigger anger, laughter, tears, or a combination of the three. At this stage, the facilitator has no idea what triggers a specific emotion for anyone in the room. But that's okay because now each attendee has been positioned to start discovering that for themselves and becoming responsible for their feelings and own the actions triggered by those emotions.

Growth is ready to begin. Most of the steps give clues that each of us may use to keep growing.

Chapter 17

Annotate and Identify the Triggers

Once identified, they can be named and tamed.

You alone are the only person who can recognize your triggers—and it is *important* that you pay attention to them. Once you own your emotions, understand the trigger concept, and train yourself to identify the triggers and control the results through foundational, fact-based thinking, you will gradually become free of garbage.

Will it be gone? No. But each time you act responsibly, it will be less of a force on your life.

Surviving Your Feelings

Returning to the group setting of my "Surviving Your Feelings" presentations, have each person make their own picture of the ribbed bucket described in the previous chapter. Have them draw a lid with latches and valves to show the strength the bucket needs to keep the nasty garbage contained. Then add pipes with funnels to depict how to insert all the garbage that collects within, pressurized by the input pump and from the bilge.

Ask, "What happens next?"

Someone will likely respond, "It leaks or explodes." Then ask, "What causes that to happen?" Discuss how wrong moves cause pain and how that pain colors life in general.

As various answers come in, note them for comparison. Then ask:

- What does it take to make the can explode? Is it strong emotion?
- Could one, small trigger pop the lid?
- Does it have to be a single, major bad item? Maybe it's a good item that causes us to drive ourselves into a corner of tears or to explode on someone.
- What can we do with the contents that aren't destructive?

Annotate and Identify the Triggers

- Can we solve this problem alone? Why or why not?
- What makes solving this dilemma so hard?
- Do you have any historical ideas we might look toward for solutions?

Discuss their responses—for they are now ready to start disarming their bucket of garbage. The above steps can also be done by using the "as is" chart mentioned in the next chapter.

Chapter 18

Disarming the Explosive Garbage Can

Identify fears, drop untruths, look, and see.

The Christian disciple, Paul, once wrote in the Soul Maintenance Handbook, "Remember this: nothing will happen to you but what is common to people." He also wrote that the temptations in your life are no different from what others experience.

Compare what Paul wrote to the answers compiled

in the previous chapter. Where can we go to find and read good results based on truth? Library shelves are filled with truths and facts just waiting to be discovered. Carefully sort the truths from impulsive, self-centered emotions.

For most of us, the reality is that we are all in the same boat—and the bilge water can get really nasty, and it will stay that way, until we pump out the slime.

How do we disarm the garbage can? We can seldom do it alone. Find someone you can trust and confess your fears and failures to one another. Once you understand how alike you are in carrying emotional garbage, you can ask questions of one another and weigh your answers without condemnation or keeping score. As you do, listen for replies that build up, but do not condone, condemn, or destroy—and never allow the "Oh, you poor baby" concept to enter the conversation.

People who can discuss anything can *solve* anything, even if it hurts or leads to triggers that have to be dealt with. They are immeasurably valuable!

After working with someone to get to the leveling point where you can look at one another with value,

Disarming the Explosive Garbage Can

assess what it cost to get there? Would you return to the dark side? Would you give some treasure to get where you are now?

Another effective tool is to draw an "as is" chart. All it takes is a sheet of paper with a vertical line drawn down the middle of the page. At the top of one side, write "Positive or Growth." On the other side, write "Negative or Failure." Put an item or two on each appropriate side, and list the triggers and results for each item. Ask yourself:

- What works well in my life?
- What areas fail?
- How can I know the difference between the two?

Then jot down good or bad side factors for each one that can be used to counteract or implement action. After listing all the pros and cons, ask yourself, "Where am I?" Look for positive, truth-based tools to replace negative, lie-based influences that will help you move from where you are to where you want to be.

If you are in a group setting like the one described earlier, ask:

Surviving Your Feelings

- What was the most important idea identified by the group once they realized they were not alone in carrying their can of emotional garbage?
- What happened when we looked at someone else who was in the same boat?
- Did we get stronger or weaker with this exposure?
- What are the successful actions we revealed to handle the results of this exposure?
- What was the most important factor in sorting truthful tools from broken ones?
- Is there any way we can explain what has taken place here to an individual who has never experienced the value of revealing the universality of truth? Why may they not hear it?
- What will the walls look and sound like?
- What will their replies sound like?
- Might you hear justifications or "Yeah, but…?"

You are discovering how to disarm the garbage can! Again, you cannot run from a crisis. Deal with it! Do not deny or blame. Solve it.

Chapter 19

Building Blocks or Roadblocks?

**How you approach them determines
how you leave them.**

Truth is so much larger than emotions. Yet negative emotions left in charge will never allow truth to arrive. Harmful emotions collect around fears and can change instantly. Anxiety, stress, and exposure create a level of pain in anticipation of the truth, so truth is denied because it brings us too dangerously close to the pit of garbage. But worse pain comes from the anticipation of more nasty or fearful emotions that never seem to go away. We may feel surrounded.

Those emotional roadblocks, however, cannot destroy truth. Truths that are identified and used to conquer fear become a comfortable refuge, providing building blocks that will sooner or later overcome the garbage. Each block can provide a better view forward.

How might you try to share success in surviving your feelings apart from facilitated group discussion?

1. Come upon a person with a full bucket that expresses a need to step out.
2. Seek a friend or a leader who will be truthful enough to gently expose failing behaviors.
3. Find a counselor who can engage without demanding a "right" answer.

I call this approach "triad" counseling: matching dangerous behaviors to emotional responses from life's triggers.

One-on-one counseling alone can be slow and difficult, and it is hard because, when the person with the full bucket goes out the door, they can tend

Building Blocks or Roadblocks?

to leave ownership of their bucket behind and may never follow up with the problem solving insights they received from the counseling. In a word, this is often called deniability. However, "triad" counseling makes it nearly impossible for someone to leave it behind. Just as in a group, they now know two people they can look in the eye without fear of exposure. They know that "what is said here stays here," and that foundation of accountability and vulnerability becomes a firm place to build strength.

These "triad" sessions are longer and take a little more patience, but when the person fills their "as is" sheet, labels the trigger buttons, and identifies good and bad behaviors, they rapidly drop much of the "stuff and bluff" and get cleaner inside. They discover strength worth emulating, honesty worth seeking, and trustworthiness so valuable as to be treasured.

Chapter 20

The Cafeteria of Life

Life demands steps to start. Tough and long enough to stretch us, yet short enough to provide visible, safe progress.

Life will deliver everything under the sun: good, bad, happy, sad, tickled pink, and hurtful as can be. We must take what comes and deal with it all. Picture yourself leaving a small, warm place through a hard-to-move little door, and then you are instantly hit with a cold breeze. Next, you see another little glass door. That is today's door, and it seems to have something beyond it that you must take for today. You go through it to find yourself before a sliding glass door that enters into the Cafeteria of Life.

Every day presents a new door to open that can sustain or challenge you, but that will never take you backwards. You always proceed forward in life, and each new day has a treasure or load to carry through it. So, onward you go, bearing much, fearing some, and listening to gentle directions that seem to fill your space with passing comforts. You come to larger spaces with more tasks, tests, pleasures, and discomforts, all of which trigger varied sensations. Some doors may seem difficult to go through because of the burdens you are carrying, yet you carry on until you come to the room with a familiar container—the one filled with the garbage of life.

But you are not dissuaded. Why? Because you've learned what to do. You disarm the explosive fuse on the can, free yourself of your negative burdens, and proceed into the light. It shines with a glow you have never conceived or dreamed of in your life.

The light of freedom!

When we dump our emotional garbage daily, we are reborn to another venue of life that is solidly

The Cafeteria of Life

beautiful, truthful, honorable, and most delightful to enter into.

The Cafeteria of Life has two immutable rules. 1) You must take everything life has handed you. 2) You cannot go back but must always move on. Much must be taken with you or handled by you, but at the end of the day, you can either keep the garbage and let it eat away at you, or you can dump it and live in sweet freedom.

It's your choice.

It is *always* your choice.

Chapter 21

Freedom with Responsibility

Freedom with no specific limits is a trap.

True freedom is experienced by choosing the things of a successful life by using tested values based upon proven truths. This requires you to take the responsibility to act with these truths in mind, always being as gentle as possible and only as strong as is necessary to protect yourself and others from those who are less equipped to experience life with truth, candor, and trustworthiness.

Remember, deal with it now, act with everything

as it comes, use the good stuff, and dump the bad stuff. You cannot touch yesterday; you cannot reach tomorrow. All you have is *now*. That's a vital fact that positions you to face every moment of every day while surviving your feelings and enjoying true freedom.

Each value presented in the Soul Maintenance Handbook I've mentioned throughout this book is simple, testable, and historically usable. You will experience obvious results from following (or ignoring) its admonitions. Every value is justified by the results of your behavior. Successful behaviors need no explanation and will do no harm.

I close with a single request. Try the ideas presented in *Surviving Your Feelings* and apply them to your life for 90 days. If they do not provide valuable guidance to enjoy more of your life, please let me know and tell me what needs to be added, subtracted, or changed with proven, tested, and truthful sources. If this material has assisted you and yours in any way, it would be nice to know that as well.

Finally, I realize there is a strong possibility that I have offended someone with my statements and observations. Please forgive me. My intent was *not* to offend. My sole hope was to give you direction toward a happier, fulfilling life. Several thousand people have been exposed to the ideas presented here, and not a single person rejected the ideas given. A large and uncounted number of people have returned with praise for having gained the tools to clean up their cookie jar (formerly their garbage can).

About the Author

Dennis C. Stager was born in Kalamazoo, Michigan and raised in the farming community of Galesburg, Michigan. After graduating from Galesburg-Augusta High School in 1956, he joined the United States Navy. The following years took him all over the world and to many interesting places. This expanded the observational skills that were most useful in helping him have a successful military career, often fulfilling jobs far outside the technical side of aviation electronics.

Dennis spent nearly 29 years in the U.S. Navy Aviation Branch, Technical Aviation Electronics,

Surviving Your Feelings

from 1956-1990. Limited broken service time was spent attending college for three years of premed courses followed by two-to-four year tours of dedicated instructor duty teaching technical avionics courses, maintenance administration, and quality control. He taught instructors how to teach many of these skill areas. Dennis also facilitated and team taught a successful racial relations program.

Designated as a Navy Master Training Specialist on each instructor tour (a title that, at that time, was not widely bestowed), Dennis developed a course on alcohol/drug recovery and taught a facilitated foundational program called "Surviving Your Feelings." He was sought by various outside commands for leadership venues, pre-promotion training, relationship counseling, and so on.

In addition, Dennis became a civilian commercial pilot and flight instructor, and he taught a Sunday School for adults using the Socratic method of teaching that utilizes hundreds of questions to provide knowledge for all attendees and promote their social growth. Dennis has been a drug/alcohol and marriage counselor, a guest speaker on aviation safety

About the Author

and leadership for all grades and ranks, and he has conducted healing memorial services.

Dennis received much recognition for his accomplishments outside of his assigned duties in the military, earning Navy Achievement medals, a Navy Commendation medal, and yearly evaluations annotating his skill at identifying problems in technical or personnel areas, seeking solutions, and implementing them.

As a writer, Dennis wrote many maintenance and instruction manual changes to improve results by applying the skills learned in classroom or work environments, and he wrote an article for Navy Aviation Safety magazine highlighting the often invisible dangers of high pressure hydraulic leaks and the serious medical effects of possible body contamination from aircraft fluids. Finally, Dennis has received two awards from the Freedom Foundation for humanity letters supporting human behaviors for success.

During their many travels, Dennis and his spouse, Virginia, have opened their doors to single folks isolated from home and to others with various injuries, or to shipmates and social acquaintances who were just nice to have around. Their home is dedicated to sharing life with no score keeping. They currently live in Arizona, still enjoy working with people, and are enjoying their retirement while writing as a hobby.

You can email Dennis at dcndes43@gmail.com

www.ingramcontent.com/pod-product-compliance
Lightning Source LLC
Chambersburg PA
CBHW071134090426
42736CB00012B/2120